©2005 Algrove Publishing Limited
ALL RIGHTS RESERVED.
No part of this book may be reproduced in any form, including photocopying, without permission in writing from the publishers, except by a reviewer who may quote brief passages in a magazine or newspaper or on radio or television.

Algrove Publishing Limited
36 Mill Street, P.O. Box 1238
Almonte, Ontario, Canada K0A 1A0

Telephone: (613) 256-0350
Fax: (613) 256-0360
Email: sales@algrove.com

Library and Archives Canada Cataloguing in Publication

Williams, J. R. (James Robert), 1888-1957.
    Out our way sampler, 20s, 30s & 40s / J.R. Williams.

(Classic reprint series)
ISBN 1-897030-33-9

American wit and humor, Pictorial. I. Title. II. Series: Classic reprint series (Almonte, Ont.)

NC1429.W573A4 2005d   741.5'973   C2005-904386-5

Printed in Canada
#1-8-05

Publisher's Note

J.R. Williams drew over 10,000 cartoons in his life, the vast majority under the *Out Our Way* heading. We have sampled the 22 years of his work here so that you can see the evolution of his style.

Earlier we produced thematic books of his cartoons covering all of his cowboy, cavalry and machine shop humor. The cartoons in this volume are almost entirely of family life or social situations, the main body of his work.

We expect to produce additional volumes of *Out Our Way* in the future but much depends on the reception of this volume. It is difficult for us to be objective about Williams since we have become mesmerized by his work. The market will tell us whether or not publishing future volumes would be wise.

Leonard G. Lee, Publisher
Almonte, Ontario
August 2005

How We Make Our Books - *You may not have noticed, but this book is quite different from other softcover books you might own. The vast majority of paperbacks, whether mass-market or the more expensive trade paperbacks, have the pages sheared and notched at the spine so that they may be glued together. The paper itself is often of newsprint quality. Over time, the paper will brown and the spine will crack if flexed. Eventually the pages fall out.*

All of our softcover books, like our hardcover books, have sewn bindings. The pages are sewn in signatures of sixteen or thirty-two pages and these signatures are then sewn to each other. They are also glued at the back but the glue is used primarily to hold the cover on, not to hold the pages together.

We also use only acid-free paper in our books. This paper does not yellow over time. A century from now, this book will have paper of its original color and an intact binding, unless it has been exposed to fire, water, or other catastrophe.

There is one more thing you will note about this book as you read it; it opens easily and does not require constant hand pressure to keep it open. In all but the smallest sizes, our books will also lie open on a table, something that a book bound only with glue will never do unless you have broken its spine.

The cost of these extras is well below their value and while we do not expect a medal for incorporating them, we did want you to notice them.

Out Our Way
Sampler
20s, 30s & 40s

THE GREAT
WHITE DESERT.

J.R.WILLIAMS

Algrove Publishing
Classic Reprint Series

Table of Contents

OUT OUR WAY 1922 1

OUT OUR WAY 1923 19

OUT OUR WAY 1924 37

OUT OUR WAY 1925 55

OUT OUR WAY 1926 73

OUT OUR WAY 1927 91

OUT OUR WAY 1928 109

OUT OUR WAY 1929 127

OUT OUR WAY 1930 145

OUT OUR WAY 1931 163

OUT OUR WAY 1932 181

OUT OUR WAY 1933 199

OUT OUR WAY 1934 217

OUT OUR WAY 1935 235

OUT OUR WAY 1936 253

OUT OUR WAY 1937 271

OUT OUR WAY 1938 289

OUT OUR WAY 1939 307

OUT OUR WAY 1940 325

OUT OUR WAY 1941 343

OUT OUR WAY 1942 361

OUT OUR WAY 1943 379

IMPROVING
HIS CLAIM

This may not look like a kitchen sink today but that is what one looked like in 1922.

Many major scrap metal businesses started out with an immigrant working with only a horse and cart.

ELF DAKIN HAS TO BE MIGHTY CAREFUL WHO HE SITS BEHIND WHEN HE GOES TO THE MOVIES.

AMBITION

J.R.WILLIAMS

THE BOUGHT'N HAIRCUT.

THE WINDUP

FIRESIDE ESSAYS.

MODESTY OF THE TALENTED.

THE PERFECT GENTLEMAN.

THE TELL TAIL

J.P.WILLIAMS

THE FORGER.

J.P.WiLLiAMS

WINDOW PAINS.

J.R.WILLIAMS

THE TORTURE CHAMBER

A BREATH OF THE GREAT OUTDOORS.

J.R.WILLIAMS

HOW THE OLD HOMESTEAD LOOKS BY THE
TIME A FELLOW CAN AFFORD TO BUY IT.

THE FIRST LONG PANTS

THE DIVIDING LINE

THROUGH A MOTHERS EYES.

THE HANDWRITING EXPERT.

AND THEY DO

DRAWING FOUR PER CENT
INTEREST ON A BANK.

J.R.WILLIAMS

THE BUSINESS END OF A COLLEGE YEAR.

GARDEN BUGS

A SOCIAL DOWNFALL

J.P.WILLIAMS

A SEAT OF LEARNING.

BREATHLESS MOMENTS
HERE HE COMES!

J.P.Williams

HEROES ARE MADE - NOT BORN.

WHEN SEEING ISNT BELIEVING

J.R.WiLLiAMS

"THE THINKER"-
SUPPER TIME AND ABOUT A -
HUNDRED MORE BILLS TO PASS

J.R.WILLIAMS

THE UPLIFTERS

GOOD MEDICINE AND BAD.

ECONOMIC TRANSPOPTATION.

A CLOSE RELATION

J.R.WILLIAMS

GOOD MEDICINE AND BAD.

WHY MOTHERS GET GRAY.

WHY MOTHERS GET GRAY-
A LIGHT LUNCH.

J.R.WILLIAMS

WHY MOTHERS GET GRAY
THE LOOKOUT.

J.R.WiLLiAMS

HEROES ARE MADE – NOT BORN.

HEROES ARE MADE - NOT BORN.

SYMPATHY

HEROES ARE MADE - NOT BORN.

THE POST MORTEM.

THE OLD CROSSING WATCHMAN WASN'T QUITE AS WOBBLY AS THE BOYS THOUGHT HE'D BE AFTER SUCH A LONG ILLNESS.

WHY MOTHERS GET GRAY —
COMIN' IN ON A WILD THROW.

J.P.WILLIAMS

MOMENTS WE'D LIKE TO LIVE OVER
THE GULLIBLE PUBLIC

WHY MOTHERS GET GRAY—
FAMILY SECRETS.

Castor oil was the universal purgative and lubricant for more than a century.

MOMENTS WE'D LIKE TO LIVE OVER—
THE LAST OF THE "LITTLE LORD FAUNTLEROYS

MOMENTS WE'D LIKE TO LIVE OVER -
NEW KID IN THE NEIGHBORHOOD

HIS BROTHER'S KEEPER.

MOMENTS WE'D LIKE TO LIVE OVER—
THE BEST MA IN THE WHOLE WORLD.

In a cold bedroom a flat-iron wrapped in a towel was luxury.

WHY MOTHERS GET GRAY.

HEROES ARE MADE-NOT BORN.

MOMENTS WE'D LIKE TO LIVE OVER—
HOUSE FULL OF COMPANY.

WHY MOTHERS GET GRAY.

HARDSHIP.

J.R.WILLIAMS

Carbon rods from early street lights doubled as pencils.

HEROES ARE MADE—NOT BORN.

J.R.WILLIAMS

SOWING THE SEED OF EQUAL RIGHTS

J.R.WILLIAMS

WHY MOTHERS GET GRAY

J.R.WiLLiAMS

It was once believed that baby teeth should be pulled at home using only a string.

WHY MOTHERS GET GRAY —
THE SILENT BATTLE

WHY MOTHERS GET GRAY.

J.P.WiLLIAMS

WHEN EVERY FAMILY HAD A JOKE BOOK.

J.R.WILLIAMS

INSIDE ASSISTANCE

THE OLD KITCHEN STOVE. HOW COME WE STILL LOVE THOSE OLD THINGS THAT CAUSED US SO MUCH MISERY?

A LOST ART.

HEROES ARE MADE—NOT BORN.

MOMENTS WE'D LIKE TO LIVE OVER —
THE WONDER OF THE AGE.

J.R.WILLIAMS

MOMENTS WE'D LIKE TO LIVE OVER.
HAPPY DAY.

HEROES ARE MADE - NOT BORN.

MAY MADNESS.

WHY MOTHERS GET GRAY.

J.R.WILLIAMS

MOMENTS WE'D LIKE TO LIVE OVER
HOT FOOT'N

HEROES ARE MADE - NOT BORN.

WHY MOTHERS GET GRAY.

WHY MOTHERS GET GRAY.

HEROES ARE MADE—NOT BORN

A DARK SECRET.

J.P.WILLIAMS

MOMENTS WE'D LIKE TO LIVE OVER —
OUT AT THE HEELS.

HEROES ARE MADE ~ NOT BORN.

J.R.WILLIAMS

ETHER

J.R.WILLIAMS

HEROES ARE MADE-NOT BORN — THE FINEST
WALLOW IN TOWN RIGHT IN FRONT OF YOUR HOUSE

J.R.WILLIAMS

WHEN YOU HAD THE LEAST YOU HAD THE MOST.

THE TRAMP.

FORCE DRAFT.

J.R.WILLIAMS

THE OLD BOARD WALKS

EARLY SPRING PLANTING.

WHY MOTHERS GET GRAY.

BUTTER FINGERS

THE ANTIQUE COLLECTOR.

WHY MOTHERS GET GRAY.

J.R.WILLIAMS

HEROES ARE MADE ~ NOT BORN.

HEROES ARE MADE—NOT BORN.

WHEN A DIME WAS A DIME.

MOMENTS WE'D LIKE TO LIVE OVER
OUR OLD FRONT PORCH.

BIRDS OF A FEATHER

THE GOOD SAMARITAN

WHY MOTHERS GET GRAY.

WHY MOTHERS GET GRAY.

HEROES ARE MADE ~ NOT BORN.

WHY MOTHERS GET GRAY.

THE SOAK.

ANKLIN ALONG

HEROES ARE MADE — NOT BORN

THE SMACKER.

MOMENTS WE'D LIKE TO LIVE OVER

J.R.WILLIAMS

HEROES ARE MADE — NOT BORN

WHY MOTHERS GET GRAY.

THE WAITER

WHY MOTHERS GET GRAY

J.R.WILLIAMS

THE EDGE OF CIVILIZATION.

J.R.WILLIAMS

WHY MOTHERS GET GRAY
"THE HAS BEEN"

THE DROP IN THE BUCKET.

MOMENTS WE'D LIKE TO LIVE OVER
THE TOTAL LOSS.

WHY MOTHERS GET GRAY
THE HAUNTED CAMP

J.R.WILLIAMS

BUSINESS MEN.

J.R.WILLIAMS

THE PROOF READER.

J.R.WILLIAMS

WHY MOTHERS GET GRAY

WHY MOTHERS GET GRAY.

WHY MOTHERS GET GRAY

J.P.WILLIAMS

WHY MOTHERS GET GRAY
CALLING A BLUFF —

J.R.WILLIAMS

SECOND PLACE.

WHY MOTHERS GET GRAY.

HEROES ARE MADE ~ NOT BORN

HOW "LOST ARTS" ARE LOST.

PULLIN' FOR HIMSELF

WHY MOTHERS GET GRAY~IN VACATION TIME.

BORN THIRTY YEARS TOO SOON.

J.R.WILLIAMS

SO NEAR AND YET SO FAR.

KEEPING IT TO HIMSELF.

THE MODERNIST

PUTTING ON AIRS

J.R.WiLLiAMS

GETTING A LOAD OFF HIS CHEST

J.R.WILLIAMS

Before bathtubs were common, a tub of water in the kitchen on Saturday night was the weekly bath.

BORN THIRTY YEARS TOO SOON.

J.R.WILLIAMS

HIS BROTHER'S KEEPER.

J.R.WILLIAMS

BORN THIRTY YEARS TOO SOON

THE SPECK TATOR

J.P.WILLIAMS

WHY MOTHERS GET GRAY.

THE OUTLOOK

THE WORRY WART.

THE PROBLEM SETTLERS — OUT OF SCHOOL

UNDERCOVER WORK.

THE WORM TURNS

J.P.WILLIAMS

ADVANCE NOTICE.

LOOKIN' INTO THE PAST—JUS LOOKIN'

THE WORRY WART

J.R.WILLIAMS

WHY MOTHERS GET GRAY.

WHY MOTHERS GET GRAY.

HEROES ARE MADE—NOT BORN.

BORN THIRTY YEARS TOO SOON

THE WORRY WART.

Home haircuts were standard.

HEROES ARE MADE — NOT BORN.

THE TRAILER.

THE LIFE OF THE FAMILY.

HELP.

WHY MOTHERS GET GRAY

WOMEN ARE STICKING TOGETHER, AT LAST.

WHY MOTHERS GET GRAY.

HEROES ARE MADE—NOT BORN.

SNAPPING OUT OF IT.

WHY MOTHERS GET GRAY.

HEROES ARE MADE – NOT BORN.

BORN THIRTY YEARS TOO SOON. J.R.WILLIAMS

BIRDS OF A FEATHER

J.R.WiLLIAMS

BACK SEAT SUPPRESSION

J.P.WILLIAMS

BORN THIRTY YEARS TOO SOON

J.P.WILLIAMS

Home remedies (many ineffective) were very common, particularly during the depression when money was scarce.

BORN THIRTY YEARS TOO SOON

J.R.WILLIAMS

Until after WWII, most small towns had no electricity. Ice was cut and stored in insulated buildings for summer use in ice-boxes that stored perishables.

THREE'S A CROWD

HEROES ARE MADE—NOT BORN.

MYSTERIES OF LIFE

THE REBEL

THE REFLECTION

THE HONEY MOAN

WHY MOTHERS GET GRAY

J.R.WILLIAMS

THE BIG HELP.

Horsehair was once used to stuff couches. Ends of the hair would work their way through the fabric and irritate the user.

WHY MOTHERS GET GRAY

WHY MOTHERS GET GRAY

THE WORRY WART.

MORE THAN LIKELY

THE WORRY WART

THE NEAR GREAT

J.R.WILLIAMS

THE SPRING TONIC

THE TENNIS RACKET

THE GENTLEMAN

BORN THIRTY YEARS TOO SOON

WHY MOTHERS GET GRAY

THE DAINTY

J.P.WILLIAMS

WHY MOTHERS GET GRAY

J.R.WiLLiams

THE GO-GETTERS

A PERFECT LIKENESS.

J.R.WILLIAMS

WHY MOTHERS GET GRAY.

J.P.Williams

WHY MOTHERS GET GRAY.

WHY MOTHERS GET GRAY.

THE FAMILIAR TOUCH.

WHY MOTHERS GET GRAY.

J.P.WILLIAMS

WHY MOTHERS GET GRAY.

QUICK RETURNS.

THE RUBBER DUCK.

J.P.WiLLiAMS

WHY MOTHERS GET GRAY.

WHY MOTHERS GET GRAY

The boy is carrying a kerosene can. Kerosene was the usual lamp fuel before electricity.

WHY MOTHERS GET GRAY.

WHY MOTHERS GET GRAY.

J.P.WiLLiAMS

BORN THIRTY YEARS TOO SOON.

THE HANG-OUT   J.P.WILLIAMS

BORN THIRTY YEARS TOO SOON.

WHY MOTHERS GET GRAY

HEROES ARE MADE — NOT BORN

TIMING

J.P.WILLIAMS

STICKING THE TEACHER

WHY MOTHERS GET GRAY

J.R.WILLIAMS

THE WATER SAVERS

WHY MOTHERS GET GRAY

Good housekeepers kept the top of their cookstoves shiny black using stove blacking, carbon in a grease base.

WHY MOTHERS GET GRAY

J.R.WILLIAMS

WHY MOTHERS GET GRAY

BORN THIRTY YEARS TOO SOON.   J.R.WILLIAMS

YOUNG IZAAK WALTON

J.R.WILLIAMS

Izaak Walton wrote "The Compleat Angler".

THE SCAIRT SCARERS

J.R.WILLIAMS

HEROES ARE MADE – NOT BORN

J.P.WiLLiAMS

WHY MOTHERS GET GRAY

THE DOUBLE

J.P.WILLIAMS

THE JOKER

J.P.WILLIAMS.

WHY MOTHERS GET GRAY

THE RUNNING MATE

J.R.WILLIAMS

WHY MOTHERS GET GRAY

PROOF OF THE WOODEN

WHY MOTHERS GET GRAY

J.R.WILLIAMS

WOODEN WONDER

J.P.WILLIAMS

WHY MOTHERS GET GRAY

WHY MOTHERS GET GRAY

WHY MOTHERS GET GRAY

WHY MOTHERS GET GRAY

WHY MOTHERS GET GRAY

J.R.WILLIAMS

SHORTCOMINGS

WHY MOTHERS GET GRAY

BORN THIRTY YEARS TOO SOON

THE TOURIST

J.P.WiLLIAMS

THE WORRY WART

J.P.WILLIAMS

WHY MOTHERS GET GRAY

BORN THIRTY YEARS TOO SOON

THE SHAVER

WHY MOTHERS GET GRAY

BORN THIRTY YEARS TOO SOON

J.P.WILLIAMS

THE BLACK SHEEP

WHY MOTHERS GET GRAY

THE VEST PROTECTOR

WHY MOTHERS GET GRAY

THE WORRY WART

BORN THIRTY YEARS TOO SOON

WHY MOTHERS GET GRAY

WHY MOTHERS GET GRAY

J.R.WILLIAMS

WHY MOTHERS GET GRAY

HEROES ARE MADE—NOT BORN

AND HIM, TOO

WHY MOTHERS GET GRAY

HEROES ARE MADE - NOT BORN

THE WORRY WART

WHY MOTHERS GET GRAY

THE WORRY WART.

THE BLINDFOLDS

J.R.WiLLiAMS

THE WORRY WART

J.R.WILLIAMS

THE FLOWING TIE

J.R.WILLIAMS

THE SPILLWAY

Stoves were often moved from inside to a summer kitchen, an uninsulated addition, for the hot months.

WHY MOTHERS GET GRAY

SURGERY

J.P.WILLIAMS

WHY MOTHERS GET GRAY

THE CUSHION TREAD

J.R.WILLIAMS

GOOD MEDICINE AND BAD

HEROES ARE MADE- NOT BORN

BORN THIRTY YEARS TOO SOON

BORN THIRTY YEARS TOO SOON

Ashes were commonly sifted to recover any pieces of unburned coal.

THE RAMROD

THE BALLAST

AND NO LEAKS EITHER

THE MIDDLE MAN

Even children were expected to buy war bonds with their pocket money.

WHY MOTHERS GET GRAY.

Early barber shops were often informal mens' clubs. Not everyone was there for a haircut.

THE CAMP

HEROES ARE MADE – NOT BORN

During WWII there were frequent drives for scrap metal. Even bones were collected to be ground for fertilizer.

THE SEAMY SIDE

J.R.WILLIAMS

SPRING PERFUMES

J.P.WILLIAMS

THE WELCOME SACRIFICE

WHY MOTHERS GET GRAY

THE LONG AND SHORTAGE

THE EMANCIPATORS

THE TRICKSTERS

J.P.WILLIAMS

J.R.WILLIAMS   THE COCOON

THE INSURANCE

J.R.WILLIAMS

THE AWFUL SACRIFICE

J.R.WILLIAMS

THE ROUND TRIP   J.R.WILLIAMS

THE PASSPORT

WHY MOTHERS GET GRAY   J.P.WiLLIAMS

Stomping around on shaky old wooden floors could cause a cake to fall as it was baking.

TRAILER TROUBLE   J.P.WILLIAMS

CAMOUFLAGE   J.R.WILLIAMS

WHY MOTHERS GET GRAY

WHY MOTHERS GET GRAY   J.R.WiLLiAMS

THE MODERN "TOUCHED"

If you are a fan of J.R. Williams, you may be
interested in our other Williams Classic Reprints.

Classic Cowboy Cartoons

U.S. Cavalry Cartoons

The Bull of the Woods

Publications by Algrove Publishing Limited

The following is a list of titles from our popular *"Classic Reprint Series"* as well as other publications by Algrove Publishing Limited.

ARCHITECTURE, BUILDING, AND DESIGN

Item #	Title
49L8038	A BOOK OF ALPHABETS WITH PLAIN, ORNAMENTAL, ANCIENT AND MEDIAEVAL STYLES
49L8096	A GLOSSARY OF TERMS USED IN ENGLISH ARCHITECTURE
49L8016	BARN PLANS & OUTBUILDINGS
49L8046	BEAUTIFYING THE HOME GROUNDS
49L8112	BUILDING WITH LOGS AND LOG CABIN CONSTRUCTION
49L8092	DETAIL, COTTAGE AND CONSTRUCTIVE ARCHITECTURE
49L8015	FENCES, GATES & BRIDGES
49L8706	FROM LOG TO LOG HOUSE
49L0720	HOMES & INTERIORS OF THE 1920'S
49L8111	LOW-COST WOOD HOMES
49L8030	SHELTERS, SHACKS & SHANTIES
49L8050	STRONG'S BOOK OF DESIGNS
49L8064	THE ARCHITECTURE OF COUNTRY HOUSES
49L8021	THE INTERNATIONAL CYCLOPEDIA OF MONOGRAMS
49L8023	THE OPEN TIMBER ROOFS OF THE MIDDLE AGES

CLASSIC CATALOGS

Item #	Title
49L8004	BOULTON & PAUL, LTD. 1898 CATALOGUE
49L8098	CATALOG OF MISSION FURNITURE 1913 – *COME-PACKT FURNITURE*
49L8097	MASSEY-HARRIS CIRCA 1914 CATALOG
49L8089	OVERSHOT WATER WHEELS FOR SMALL STREAMS
49L8079	WILLIAM BULLOCK & CO. – *HARDWARE CATALOG CIRCA 1850*

GARDENING

Item #	Title
49L8082	CANADIAN WILD FLOWERS (C. P. TRAILL)
49L8113	COLLECTING SEEDS OF WILD PLANTS AND SHIPPING LIVE PLANT MATERIAL
49L8029	FARM WEEDS OF CANADA
49L8056	FLORA'S LEXICON
49L8705	REFLECTIONS ON THE FUNGALOIDS
49L8076	THE WILDFLOWERS OF AMERICA
49L8057	THE WILDFLOWERS OF CANADA

HUMOR AND PUZZLES

Item #	Title
49L8074	ARE YOU A GENIUS? WHAT IS YOUR I.Q?
49L8106	CLASSIC COWBOY CARTOONS, VOL. 1
49L8109	CLASSIC COWBOY CARTOONS, VOL. 2
49L8118	CLASSIC COWBOY CARTOONS, VOL. 3
49L8119	CLASSIC COWBOY CARTOONS, VOL. 4
49L8072	CLASSIC PUZZLES AND HOW TO SOLVE THEM
49L8103	GRANDMOTHER'S PUZZLE BOOK
49L8081	MR. PUNCH WITH ROD AND GUN – *THE HUMOUR OF FISHING AND SHOOTING*
49L8073	NAME IT! THE PICTORIAL QUIZ BOOK
49L8126	OUR BOARDING HOUSE WITH MAJOR HOOPLE – *1927*
49L8125	OUT OUR WAY – *SAMPLER 20s, 30s & 40s*
49L8044	SAM LOYD'S PICTURE PUZZLES
49L8071	THE BULL OF THE WOODS, VOL. 1
49L8080	THE BULL OF THE WOODS, VOL. 2
49L8104	THE BULL OF THE WOODS, VOL. 3
49L8114	THE BULL OF THE WOODS, VOL. 4
49L8115	THE BULL OF THE WOODS, VOL. 5
49L8116	THE BULL OF THE WOODS, VOL. 6
49L8084	THE ART OF ARTHUR WATTS
49L8107	U.S. CAVALRY CARTOONS

NAVAL AND MARINE

Item #	Title
49L8090	BOAT-BUILDING AND BOATING
49L8707	BUILDING THE NORWEGIAN SAILING PRAM *(MANUAL AND PLANS)*
49L8708	BUILDING THE SEA URCHIN *(MANUAL AND PLANS)*
49L8078	MANUAL OF SEAMANSHIP FOR BOYS AND SEAMEN OF THE ROYAL NAVY, 1904
49L8095	SAILING SHIPS AT A GLANCE
49L8099	THE SAILOR'S WORD-BOOK
49L8058	THE YANKEE WHALER
49L8025	THE YOUNG SEA OFFICER'S SHEET ANCHOR
49L8061	TRADITIONS OF THE NAVY

REFERENCE

Item #	Title
49L8083	AMERICAN MECHANICAL DICTIONARY – KNIGHT VOL. I, VOL. II, VOL. III
49L8093	507 MECHANICAL MOVEMENTS
49L8024	1800 MECHANICAL MOVEMENTS AND DEVICES
49L8055	970 MECHANICAL APPLIANCES AND NOVELTIES OF CONSTRUCTION
49L8602	ALL THE KNOTS YOU NEED
49L8077	CAMP COOKERY
49L8001	LEE'S PRICELESS RECIPES
49L8018	THE BOY'S BOOK OF MECHANICAL MODELS
49L8019	WINDMILLS AND WIND MOTORS

TRADES

Item #	Title
49L8014	BOOK OF TRADES
49L8086	FARM BLACKSMITHING
49L8031	FARM MECHANICS
49L8087	FORGING
49L8027	HANDY FARM DEVICES AND HOW TO MAKE THEM
49L8002	HOW TO PAINT SIGNS & SHO' CARDS
49L8054	HOW TO USE THE STEEL SQUARE
49L8094	THE YOUNG MILL-WRIGHT AND MILLER'S GUIDE
49L8053	THE METALWORKING LATHE

WOODWORKING AND CRAFTS

Item #	Title
49L8101	ARTS-CRAFTS LAMPS & SHADES – *HOW TO MAKE THEM*
49L8012	BOY CRAFT
49L8110	CHAIN SAW AND CROSSCUT SAW TRAINING COURSE
49L8048	CLAY MODELLING AND PLASTER CASTING
49L8005	COLONIAL FURNITURE
49L8065	COPING SAW WORK
49L8032	DECORATIVE CARVING, PYROGRAPHY AND FLEMISH CARVING
49L8091	FURNITURE DESIGNING AND DRAUGHTING
49L8049	HANDBOOK OF TURNING
49L8020	MISSION FURNITURE, HOW TO MAKE IT
49L8033	ORNAMENTAL AND DECORATIVE WOOD CARVINGS
49L8059	PROJECTS FOR WOODWORK TRAINING
49L8003	RUSTIC CARPENTRY
49L8085	SKELETON LEAVES AND PHANTOM FLOWERS
49L8068	SPECIALIZED JOINERY
49L8052	STANLEY COMBINATION PLANES – *THE 45, THE 50 & THE 55*
49L8034	THE ART OF WHITTLING
49L8047	TIMBER – *FROM THE FOREST TO ITS USE IN COMMERCE*
49L8042	TURNING FOR AMATEURS
49L8039	VIOLIN MAKING AS IT WAS, AND IS
49L8013	YOU CAN MAKE IT
49L8035	YOU CAN MAKE IT FOR CAMP & COTTAGE
49L8036	YOU CAN MAKE IT FOR PROFIT
49L8067	WOOD HANDBOOK – *WOOD AS AN ENGINEERING MATERIAL*
49L8060	WOODEN PLANES AND HOW TO MAKE THEM

Algrove Publishing Limited, 36 Mill Street, P.O. Box 1238, Almonte, Ontario, Canada K0A 1A0
Telephone: (613) 256-0350   Fax: (613) 256-0360   Email: sales@algrove.com